GYMNASTICS

Gymnastics Essentials

Safety and Equipment

by Jen Jones

Consultant
Connie Dickson
Minnesota State Chair
USA Gymnastics Women's Program

Capstone
press®

Mankato, Minnesota

Snap Books are published by Capstone Press,

151 Good Counsel Drive, P.O. Box 669, Mankato, Minnesota 56002.

www.capstonepress.com

Library of Congress Cataloging-in-Publication Data
Jones, Jen, 1976–
     Gymnastics essentials : safety and equipment / by Jen Jones.
     p. cm. — (Snap books. Gymnastics)
     Summary: "A guide for children and pre-teens on the equipment used
in gymnastics and how to keep safe while training"—Provided by publisher.
     Includes bibliographical references and index.
     ISBN-13: 978-0-7368-6468-8 (hardcover)
     ISBN-10: 0-7368-6468-7 (hardcover)
     1. Gymnastics—Juvenile literature. 2. Gymnastics—Safety measures—
Juvenile literature. I. Title. II. Series.
GV461.3.J35 2007
796.44—dc22   2006006001

Editor: Wendy Dieker
Designer: Jennifer Bergstrom
Illustrator: Renée Doyle
Photo Researcher/Photo Editor: Kelly Garvin

Photo Credits: Capstone Press/Karon Dubke, cover, 3 (all), 8–9 (left), 9 (right), 11, 13 (grips), 14–15, 16–17, 18–19,
20–21, 22–23 (all), 24–25; Getty Images Inc./AFP/MLADEN ANTONOV, 27; Getty Images Inc./AFP/WILLIAM WEST,
29; Jennifer Jones, 32; Masterfile/Brian Pieters, 13 (left); PhotoEdit Inc./Frank Siteman, 6–7; SportsChrome Inc./
Michael Zito, 4–5

Capstone Press thanks the staff and the gymnasts at Twin City Twisters Gymnastics, Champlin, Minnesota,
for their assistance with photo shoots.

1 2 3 4 5 6 11 10 09 08 07 06

TABLE OF CONTENTS

8-9

16-17

22-23

Features

A Gymnast's Toolbox

A toolbox of safety and equipment will help you build your gymnastics career.

Watching gymnasts in motion is a thrilling experience. Gymnasts make unbelievable shapes with their bodies and fly gracefully through the air. It's hard not to admire them.

As you become more experienced, you will want to try the advanced skills that leave everyone in awe. Soon, you will be getting the same attention!

Remember that gymnastics comes with some risk. If moves are done incorrectly, gymnasts will likely seriously hurt themselves. This book will give you the tools to train safely. It's also a fun introduction to the different types of gymnastics equipment. Protect yourself from harm and use the equipment carefully. You'll have a longer, safer, and more successful gymnastics career!

1

Playing It Safe

To be the best you can be, you have to be as safe as you can be!

Making Progress

It would be great to push a button and magically be able to tumble like an Olympic medalist. But the real world of gymnastics doesn't work that way. Training for competition is a long process. It demands dedication. It demands a drive to do better.

Before you can master the tough skills, you'll need to spend time mastering the basics. Safely doing cartwheels, round-offs, and handsprings is key. The easy skills get you ready to perform the hard stuff without getting hurt.

Golden Rules

If you're impatient about getting to the "good stuff," use your practice time wisely. Follow these tips, and you're sure to be headed for gold!

* Pay attention when your coach shows you moves.
* Ask questions.
* Cooperate with other students.
* Don't give up when you don't nail a move right away.

On the Spot

Motivate. Inspire. Teach. Discipline. These are things that your gymnastics coach will do for you. Your coach's role is to provide you with a complete gymnastics education. Your coach will show you the safest way to perform advanced moves. Coaches also **spot** you until you learn the moves. Spotting is when a coach gives hands-on help while you're learning a new skill. If you fall, the spotter steps in to catch you and to keep you from getting hurt.

"Go into the sport because you have fun doing it, not because of 'what ifs' and dreams of gold medals."
–Shannon Miller, U.S. Olympic medalist

In some cases, a gymnast relies too much on the spotter's help. Even though she may be able to do the skill on her own, she thinks she needs the spotter. If your coach thinks you are ready to go it solo, don't be afraid! Try to rid yourself of any mental blocks by imagining yourself doing the move perfectly. Soon enough, you'll be flipping with confidence!

Safety Starts with You

Your coach or spotter will help you master skills safely. However, it's your job to take personal responsibility for yourself and others. Take note of these tips on how to be smart about safety.

* Become familiar with the rules and layout of your gym. Don't go on the equipment unless an adult is present. Also, never walk in the space where other gymnasts are performing.

* Pay attention when a move is being demonstrated. Ask your coach questions if you don't understand proper body placement.

* Before trying a new move, check the mats to make sure they are in the right place. There should be no gaps between the mats.

* Don't go free-falling! Knowing how to fall properly makes a big difference in preventing injury. Try to spread your body out when falling. If you break the fall with only one part of your body, you may end up with a sprain or break.

Get Into Gear

In artistic gymnastics events, gymnasts often let their hands do the talking. For instance, on the vault and uneven bars, a gymnast's hands are her only contact with the equipment. All that grabbing and rubbing can be very hard on the hands. To reduce blisters and calluses, gymnasts wear hand guards, or "**grips**."

"Chalking up" is another method gymnasts use to protect their hands. Gymnasts dip their hands in a bowl of powdered chalk. The chalk cuts down on the friction created when the hands rub against the bars. Less friction means gymnasts avoid tearing their hands.

Training Tools

The biggest tool is the gym where you train. When choosing a gym, it's important to make sure that the gym is a safe place. Talk with the coaches to learn about their background and see if the classes offered are up your alley. Look around and take note. Are the floors clean? Is the training area well-lit with high ceilings? Is the equipment up-to-date? If the answer to all of those questions is "yes," the gym is likely a great learning base for you.

While training, you will use various other tools for learning. An incline mat is one helpful tool. Shaped like a long triangle, it is great for learning walkovers and handsprings. Cartwheel mats make it easy to learn cartwheels. They are marked with handprints and footprints to lead the way. Spotter mats, such as barrels, give proper form for dive rolls and backbends. Foam pits, trampolines, and climbing ropes are also common practice tools found in most training gyms.

CHAPTER 2

Fully Equipped

Find out about the "goods" for each event.

SPRINGBOARD to SUCCESS

Before 2001, gymnasts vaulted over a padded "horse." It was long and rectangular. However, its design raised safety concerns. Many gymnasts had been injured because the surface was too small.

By 2003, the vault table became the official **apparatus** for upper-level gymnasts. The larger surface reduces the risk of the hands missing the vault. The one thing that stayed the same is the springboard. Athletes sprint down the runway and launch off the springboard to the table.

16

The vaulting table
* 4 feet (1.2 meters) tall
* 3 feet (1 meter) wide
* 3 feet (1 meter) long

The runway
* 78 to 82 feet
  (24 to 25 meters) long

DID YOU KNOW?

Two of the most popular vaulting skills are named after their inventors: Haruhiro "Yamashita" and Mitsuo "Tsukahara."

Uneven Bars: Raising the Bar

Made of wood-covered fiberglass, the uneven bars sit almost 6 feet (1.8 meters) apart on top of metal frames. They are designed to give bounce and provide support as the gymnasts swing and somersault from bar to bar. The distance between the bars can be adjusted slightly. The distance depends on the level of competition and the gymnast's preference.

For safety reasons, gymnasts use their palms to hold the bars. The palms have a better grip than the fingers. When releasing or swinging from bar to bar, gymnasts let go when the bar is in their sight. This way, gymnasts avoid falling backward.

Vital Stats

The high bar
* 7 feet (2.1 meters) high

The low bar
* 5 feet (1.5 meters) high

DID YOU KNOW?

Women used to compete on the men's parallel bars. The uneven bars were introduced to complement female body types and allow for more creativity in movement.

Balance Beam: Walking a Fine Line

Like the vault, the balance beam has grown safer with age. Women first began competing on the beam in the early 1930s. At that time, the beam was only 3 inches (7.6 centimeters) wide and made out of wood. As gymnasts began performing more difficult skills, a need for better safety became clear.

The modern balance beam is covered with **suede** and padded with thick rubber. Its height is easily adjusted. Beginners often practice on a much lower beam. It is still very challenging for gymnasts to tumble and dance on the beam. However, the improved safety of today's beam allows them to feel more at ease while performing.

Vital Stats

The balance beam
* 4 feet
  (1.2 meters) high
* 4 inches
  (10 centimeters) wide
* 16 feet
  (5 meters) long

DID YOU KNOW?

Gymnasts walk with their toes pointing outward to have a wider base for balance on the beam.

The Mat: Landing Pad

Ever wanted to go on a magic carpet ride? Go for the next best thing: "the floating floor!" Floor exercise mats are known as floating floors because they are mounted on 4-inch (10-centimeter) springs. Unlike other gymnastic events, gymnasts do not take hold of anything. They use the mat as a jumping-off point for leaps and tumbling skills.

Did You Know?
Until the 1960s, the floor exercise was done on a wooden floor and was considered extremely dangerous.

Vital Stats
The floor exercise mat
* 40 feet (12 meters) wide
* 40 feet (12 meters) long

Mats also make an appearance in other gymnastics events. Special mats help soften the fall from the balance beam or uneven bars. The landing mat plays an important role for vaulters and for **dismounts** from the beam and bars.

③ Other Programs

Tramps and ribbons and rings. Find out what equipment other gymnasts use.

MORE BOUNCE to the OUNCE

Named for its spring and bounce, the word "trampoline" is taken from the Spanish word for diving board. A trampoline is a bed made of strong woven fabric and covered springs. Trampolining became an Olympic gymnastics program in 2000.

Trampolines used to be elevated several feet from the ground. Now, most trampolines at the gym are built into the floor for safety. Gymnasts stay close to the middle so they don't bounce off the trampoline.

Vital Stats

The trampoline
* 7 feet (2.1 meters) wide
* 14 feet (4.3 meters) long

The Right Rhythmic Stuff

Rhythmic gymnastics is different from other programs in that gymnasts don't tumble *on* an apparatus. Instead, they *hold* an apparatus called a prop. A rhythmic gymnast twirls, tumbles, and dances. She uses the props to make beautiful visual pictures.

About 8 inches (20 centimeters) in diameter, the colorful balls of rhythmic gymnastics are made of rubber or plastic. Gymnasts roll, bounce, and toss the balls in the air.

Like a hula hoop, the hoops do not bend and are about 3 feet (1 meter) wide. The hoops are made of plastic or wood. Gymnasts do walkovers, rolls, and other moves through the hoops.

Clubs look like skinny bowling pins and are made of wood or plastic. Some gymnasts wrap them with tape to get a better grip as they roll and twist.

Ropes have knots at both ends and are the same length as the height of the gymnast. Ropes are wound around the body and used to make shapes.

Long, flowing **ribbons** are attached to sticks. The gymnast holds the stick and makes pretty designs in the air.

27

No Girls Allowed

Just as women have their own set of gymnastics apparatus, men compete on unique equipment too.

The **parallel bars** are similar to the uneven bars in make but are directly next to each other. Men display their strength by doing handstands and other poses on top of the bars.

The **horizontal bar**, or high bar, is 9 feet (3 meters) off the ground. In between giant circles around the bar, men do daring release moves that launch them 15 feet (4.6 meters) over the bar!

When performing on the **pommel horse**, men grip the handles, or "pommels," to support their weight as they do leg circles and scissor kicks around the "horse."

The **rings** hang almost 11 feet (3.4 meters) up and are about 7 inches (17.8 centimeters) wide. Men take hold of the circles and try to keep them perfectly still. They perform moves that require extreme strength.

Men and women compete on different equipment. Yet the values and work required to succeed on each apparatus remain the same.

A commitment to applying the safety information you've learned will get you far. You're now "fully equipped" to go forth with gusto!

Glossary

apparatus (ap-uh-RAT-uhss)— equipment used in gymnastics, such as the balance beam or uneven bars

dismount (DISS-mount)—a move done to get off of an apparatus

grips (GRIPS)—pieces of leather that gymnasts wear like gloves to protect the palms of the hands; grips help gymnasts hold onto the bars better.

spot (SPOT)—to help a gymnast perform a move and be ready to catch the gymnast if she falls

suede (SWAYD)—soft leather with a velvetlike surface

Fast Facts

* Before the days of the balance beam, gymnasts needed to get creative. Friedrich Jahn, considered the father of gymnastics, practiced by balancing on large logs.

* A horse is a horse, of course! In the early 1800s, vaulting horses looked just like real horses, complete with heads and tails.

* The trampoline can launch gymnasts to new heights! In 1999, English gymnast Dominic Swaffer beat his own world record by doing 84 half-twisting forward somersaults in one minute.

Read More

Bragg, Linda Wallenberg. *Play-by-Play Gymnastics.* Play-by-Play. Minneapolis: Lerner Sports, 2000.

Herran, Joe, and Ron Thomas. *Gymnastics.* Action Sports. Philadelphia: Chelsea House, 2004.

Hughes, Morgan. *Gymnastics.* Junior Sports. Vero Beach, Fla.: Rourke, 2005.

Kalman, Bobbie, and John Crossingham. *Gymnastics in Action.* Sports in Action. New York: Crabtree, 2003.

Internet Sites

FactHound offers a safe, fun way to find Internet sites related to this book. All of the sites on FactHound have been researched by our staff.

Here's how:

1. Visit *www.facthound.com*

2. Choose your grade level.

3. Type in this book ID **0736864687** for age-appropriate sites. You may also browse subjects by clicking on letters, or by clicking on pictures and words.

4. Click on the **Fetch It** button.

Facthound will fetch the best sites for you!

About the Author

Jen Jones has been very involved in the cheerleading and gymnastics worlds since she was old enough to turn a cartwheel! Jen has several years of gymnastics training and spent seven years as a cheerleader. After college, Jen cheered and choreographed for the Chicago Lawmen semi-professional football dance team. Today Jen lives in Los Angeles and writes for publications like *Pilates Style*, *American Cheerleader*, and *Dance Spirit*. She also teaches cheerleading, dance, and Pilates classes and is a certified BalleCore instructor.

Index